M O M E N T S
T O H O L D
C L O S E

Molly Burford

THOUGHT
CATALOG
Books

THOUGHTCATALOG.COM

THOUGHT CATALOG Books

Copyright © 2023 Molly Burford.

All rights reserved. No part of this book may be reproduced or transmitted in any form or any means, electronic or mechanical, without prior written consent and permission from Thought Catalog.

Published by Thought Catalog Books, an imprint of Thought Catalog, a digital magazine owned and operated by The Thought & Expression Co. Inc., an independent media organization founded in 2010 and based in the United States of America. For stocking inquiries, contact stockists@shopcatalog.com.

Produced by Chris Lavergne and Noelle Beams
Art direction and design by KJ Parish
Circulation management by Isidoros Karamitopoulos

thoughtcatalog.com | shopcatalog.com

First Edition, Limited Edition Pressing
Printed in the United States of America.

ISBN 978-1-949759-68-6

"I don't know a perfect person. I only know flawed people who are still worth loving."

—*John Green*

To Bruce, Bailey, Charlie, Scuppy, and Jessie
Thank you for showing me what love is.

BEINGS YOU HAVE
TO HOLD ON TO

Types Of People You Need To Hang On To, Part 1

Enthusiastic listeners. People who don't make you guess if they're mad. Direct communicators. The friend who helps you clean your room. People who are kind to those who can do nothing for them. Messy folks who repeatedly get it wrong but never stop trying to get it right anyway. Kindred spirits. Loud laughers. Pals who make the grocery store fun. Loved ones who get as excited about your success as you do. The person you feel comfortable crying in front of. Sing-in-the-car friends. People who text you to look at the moon. People who text you just to say hi. The one you've known since childhood who you can go a long time without talking to but nothing changes. Those who understand the value of holding space. The mentor who pushes you to do better because they want better for you. Patient teachers. Healers. Scrappy souls. Hard workers. Friends you can joke about hypothetical situations with for hours on end. The genuine. Anyone who leaves you feeling good afterward, not just when you're with them. People who see your fault lines and say they have them too. Anyone who came to mind as you read this. ***Hold them close. Love them hard.***

An Incomplete List Of Green Flags

People who tell tough truths in gentle ways. The little-things-oriented. Big picture thinkers. Dreamers. Deep feelers. Old souls. Young spirits. Goofballs. Those who don't make you choose between what's right for you and most convenient for them. The person who is listening to understand, not just waiting for their turn to speak. The ones you can share your fears with. Quiet good-doers. Humans who can admit when they're wrong (or when they don't know the answer to something). Folks who truly understand their privilege. People who aren't afraid to take the last slice of pizza. The friends who make you forget your phone. ***Anyone who reminds you that lovely things still exist.***

Some People Are Only Meant To Be Loved For A Little While

Think about it like this: Your favorite songs always end. The credits of your favorite movie will always roll. This book you're holding in your hands will, too, come to a close. Would you stop listening to music, would you stop watching movies, would you stop reading books just because they end? Shouldn't we treat people the same? Because maybe it's not about the longevity of the love but the quality of the time spent loving one another. After all, people change. *We* change. Who we are when we fell in love may no longer exist and vice versa. And after a little while ends with someone else, we can adore them from a distance and wish them well. Some people are only meant to be loved for a little while, and that's okay.

HOW TO CONNECT

————————————— Be vulnerable.

"What Does Vulnerability Feel Like?"

Vulnerability is inviting someone to sit next to you even though there are plenty of other seats they could choose at the party instead. Vulnerability is admitting you don't know something and saying, "*I was wrong.*" Vulnerability is giving a speech at your favorite person's funeral. Vulnerability is naked emotion. Vulnerability is letting someone see you with a mascara-painted face and defeated eyes. Vulnerability is an unlocked heart on your wrist and an open mind. Vulnerability is asking for help. Vulnerability is offering your hand, too. Vulnerability is telling someone they hurt your feelings, even though they might refuse to apologize. Vulnerability is accepting that some people will not change, no matter how much you wish they would. Vulnerability is trying again. Vulnerability is admitting, "*I want to break up.*" Vulnerability is understanding friends can shatter your heart, too. Vulnerability is realizing that family isn't just crimson. Vulnerability is saying "I love you" first. Vulnerability is sharing your first draft. Vulnerability is waiting at the doctor for any news at all. Vulnerability is hoping for the best without any evidence. Vulnerability is showing your scars. Vulnerability is revealing how those wounds came to be. Vulnerability is saying, "*I can't do this on my own.*" Vulnerability is necessary. Vulnerability is connection. ***Vulnerability is the foundation of love.***

Patchwork Beings

I still remember my first grade crush's birthday, but I'm not sure I'd recognize him if I saw him walking down the street. But every time the first of that spring month arrives, I think about him and who I was when I stuttered through sentences trying to form words. I still say "really," just like my roommate Amanda from college did, drawing out each syllable, so it's *reallllllyyyyyy* long. I always wait a second too long when the light turns green because that's what Granny told me to do to stay safe. As humans, we are patchwork beings, stitched together with all of the pieces of the people we loved or knew or were fascinated by once.

A THOUGHT ON LOVING

Love changes you.
If it didn't, what would
the point have been?

How To Love Better

Take the long way home. Enjoy the scenery. Observe the way they wake up and take note of what makes them laugh. Know when it's about them and when it's about you. Find the spectacular in the mundane. Ask them to text you when they get home, to work, to their vacation destination. Be infinitely curious about how they live their days. Take time apart. Make room on the couch. Embrace the fact you don't know what's best for them. Set boundaries. Express gratitude. Practice trust, even when it's scary (*especially* then). Keep both feet on the ground. Admit your mistakes. Accept their apologies. Throw away the scorecard. Kiss like you mean it. Ask more questions. Accept that it can be really hard to merge two paths; keep trying to anyway. Give them the aux cord. Give them the last fry. Give them the last word, even if you're *really* fucking pissed. Figure out what is worth the fight and what is not. Hold the door. Hold their hand. Hold space. Save them a seat. Notice the scattered gold flecks in their eyes. Tell them you're proud of them; tell them this often. Dance in the kitchen. Play hide-and-seek in the grocery store. Know you're lucky. Don't be hasty. Point out the dip in the sidewalk. Offer your arm. Offer your heart. Offer your world. ***Know when it's time to lovingly let go. Know when you need to hang on like hell.***

Things My Mother Taught Me

How to be patient. How to be kind (sometimes to a fault). How to be a good friend. The importance of creating art. The joy of independence. The beauty of tenderness. The healing ability of forgiveness. How reading is one of the great joys of life. The best David Bowie songs. Loyalty. Honesty. Feminist principles. How to stand up for what's right. How to apologize like I mean it. How to speak with intention. The mindset that romance is not the most important thing in life (though it's okay to want it, too). The power of the right shade of lipstick. Pride. How a bad day's antidote is doing something nice for another person. **That perfection isn't what makes someone worth loving.** *After all, she loves me.*

Things My Father Taught Me

How to laugh. How to ride a bike. How to be proud of myself. An endless appreciation for Bruce Springsteen's storytelling and Kölsch and (unfortunately) Fireball. That I should never cross a Scorpio or the street without looking both ways. The importance of hard work. The fact that feelings aren't always telling the full truth and that sometimes the best thing to do is let emotions pass through without analyzing them. That I should stop thinking so much and just allow myself to live. The joy of tailgating. How to be loyal. How to be a good friend. How to trust my own footing. The power of a perfectly-timed pun. Self-respect. Generosity. Goofiness. What pass interference means. Why I should never trust Ohio State fans. That it's okay to ask for help when I need it, and that it's okay to accept that help, too. To always order more pizza than I think I'll need. To stop giving second chances to people who don't deserve them. To enjoy the quiet. That no matter how old I get, I'll always want his advice. That I'm never as alone as I think I am. ***After all, I have him.***

What To Do When A Good Love Runs Its Course

When a good love runs its course, leave well enough alone. Stop forcing dead-end conversations. Stop trying to salvage the remains of something that once was everything you thought you needed and wanted. Stop trying to fix what isn't actually broken but rather the result of trying. Understand that sometimes beautiful things end, and there's nothing you can do but allow it. Allow it and allow it and allow it. And, finally, let go.

An Incomplete List Of Relationship Goals

Holding hands in old age. Holding the door. Holding space. Letting them know they pissed you off so you can resolve the issue *together*. Spending time apart. Celebrating life's little wins even though it's a Tuesday evening. Play. Honesty. Humor. Fighting right, not fighting to be right. Admitting mistakes. Offering your last fry. Offering a piece of your heart. Offering a hand with the dinner dishes. Gentle wake-ups on Sunday mornings. 2 AM laughing fits. Being best friends. Speaking up. Showing up. Growing up. Shared values. Just letting some shit go. Singing terribly in the car. Gratitude that you exist at the same time as them. Compassion. Commitment. Care. Surprise love notes left on the windshield. Taking candid photos of them during the moments you love them most. Hope. Healthy boundaries. Random hugs. Not expecting them to read your mind. Not trying to read their mind either. Deep conversation. Genuine connection. Tender disagreements. Seeing them as an imperfect person you feel lucky you took a chance on loving. Knowing they can't give you the moon and the stars. ***Not caring about those things because all you really want in this life is them.***

Lessons You Learn From Loving "The Wrong Person"

You learn how to ask for what you need. You also learn how to walk away when you *don't* receive what you need. Because you now know that your needs will never be too much for the right person.

You learn what you want in a partner. In loving the "wrong person," you come to realize what you value in a partnership because you see what happens in those values' absence.

You learn you can't save people. You now fully understand your role in a relationship is not saving. It is to be loving. Caring. Present. There. Nothing more, nothing less.

You learn the power of hope. You saw infinite potential in someone who ultimately could not, and would not, see it through. And that's a beautiful thing.

You learn that love isn't always enough to make something last. You can love someone and still know letting go is the right thing to do for both of you.

You learn that just because a relationship ends doesn't mean it didn't matter. All of it matters. And it always will.

You learn that there are no "wrong" people to love. There are just people we love, and sometimes it doesn't work out. It is good until suddenly it is not. The sun rises and sets. Our hopes rise and fall. We love, and eventually, we let each other go. And we learn from it all. We still grow.

How To Fall In Love Again

Take a deep breath. Open the door to the bar. Contemplate running right back out but go and take a seat across from kind eyes you know you'll never see again. Try to enjoy yourself anyway. Stumble over your words and fake laugh too many times before you realize you're not ready to be here just yet. Chug the rest of your Two Hearted and ask for the check. Pay your own tab and thank him for his time before giving him a hug goodbye. Walk to your car alone and put your head on the steering wheel and cry.

Blast "Broken Clocks" by SZA on the way back to your apartment and think about your own bad timing. How you always seem to be catching the signs a little too late or falling before someone is there to catch you.

Against your better judgment, swipe and swipe and swipe through Hinge when you crawl into bed later that night. Start to question whether this is really the only way to meet someone new. Pray to God that it's not. Detest your generation. Delete the app. Go to sleep and dream about the one who broke your heart. Wake up more tired than before.

Barrel through your workday. Decide you're just going to focus on yourself for a while, your career, your health, your dog, anything but finding love. Spend time alone; spend a lot of time alone. Stop going out on Friday nights and take longer than usual to text your friends back.

Forget who you are. Wish you were someone else. Decide

you hate him. Know you are lying to yourself but continue to lie anyway. Let him inspire the greatest rage you've ever felt. Burn yourself out as you realize that he wasn't so bad and that sometimes beautiful things just end, and there's nothing you can do about it but learn to live with that fact.

Figure out how to live with it. Give yourself a chance. Redownload Hinge. Try Bumble while you're at it. Remember that a broken heart is a sign you tried. Try again. Get ghosted. Take a break. Take your time. Swipe. Allow room for loneliness. Embrace uncertainty. Learn to sincerely enjoy your own company.

Contemplate where love goes when it leaves. Wonder if maybe it will always exist, even if it's not here right now. Have faith you'll cross paths with it again. Open your heart back up. Realize they weren't The One; realize there is no such thing as "The One" because our hearts are endlessly expansive, and there's always room for more love.

Remember how he encouraged you to stand taller, not slump so much. Smile as you remember the goofy night when you snuck the Fireball shooters into the movies. Remember how he fell asleep. Be grateful he happened. Be glad you two collided once.

Understand that time itself doesn't heal, but what we do within the passing hours does. Believe a different kind of love exists than the ones you experienced before. Accept that some love stories end, but you can still reference their pages. You can still appreciate it for what it was when it was. Take a deep breath. Open the door to the bar. Walk straight to the guy with shaggy hair and take a seat. Stay for four hours laughing until your stomach hurts. Realize this is how it starts. Hope it continues. *Feel faith that it will.*

Types Of People To Hold On To, Part 2

People who tell you tough truths in a gentle way, who don't say things cruelly just because it's "honest." People who don't start sentences with, "No offense, but…" People who are kind to those who can do nothing for them. People who call you on your bullshit in a funny way to make it easier to hear. People who will take pictures for strangers, taking shots from multiple angles. People who don't make you feel bad for wanting to call it an early night. People who make you forget your phone. People who sincerely listen to little kids, who remember how hard it was to be small and young and not taken seriously. People who always try their best to do the right thing and attempt to make it up when they fall short. People who still believe in love, even after they got their hearts broken time and time again. People who are deeply kind and do not stray from being so, even when they have every reason not to be. ***Hold them close, love them hard.***

The Best Types Of Chemistry

The electricity between the tips of your fingers and the ends of another's that you're reaching out to hold for the very first time. Someone finishing your sentence. Slap-happy car rides. Space. Wavelengths. Hugs that feel like a safe haven. The high of a resolution. Inside jokes. Shared ideas. The calm before the storm. The prickling anticipation in your veins as you drive to pick up the person you adore most from the airport. Trust. Faith. Loyalty. Accepted apologies. Graceful exits. The feeling of instantaneous connection when you meet someone new (but it feels like you've known them forever or at least in some other life). Laughing so hard with someone you can't even *look* at them because you know you'll just laugh louder. *The people who stay because you can't imagine life without each other.*

Underrated Types Of Love Stories

The ex-lovers who became the truest of friends. The love that was almost but not quite. The platonic soulmates. The barista you always flirted with in college whose name you have now forgotten (but not the way they made you feel). Your first dog. Your second dog, too. The love stories you wrote in your head. The love stories you held in your heart. The love stories you share with just yourself.

SOME TOUGH NEWS

Some people will give up on you. They're going to doubt you and dismiss you and misunderstand you. There are going to be people who consider you to be too much or not enough or nothing at all. *These are not your people.*

SOME GOOD NEWS:

There are people who are going to fight for you and with you. They will believe in you and speak up for you and be able to translate your heart. There will be people who consider you to be overflowing with goodness or a wallflower they feel so lucky they decided to water. *These are your people.*

The intimacy of…

Eye contact. Smirks across a crowded room. Raised eyebrows. Knowing glances. Witty banter. "I heard this song and thought of you." The sides of legs accidentally touching in the backseat. Dancing in front of strangers. Playful teasing. "I saved you a seat." Comfortable silences. Quiet time. Falling asleep together on the couch. "I'm so sorry." Hope. The little things. Inside jokes. Appreciation. Mutual trust. "You're my best friend." Crying in the car alone at a red light. Heart-to-hearts in dive bar bathrooms. Giving the benefit of the doubt. Giving a second chance. Giving in to a deep laugh. "I was literally just about to call you, too." Sharing books with your scribbles and notes throughout the margins. Losing your footing. "I never told another person that before." First hugs. A kiss you know will be your last. "I understand." A sense of safety. A feeling of alignment. Just knowing someone is here to stay, even though you have no real evidence for thinking so. ***Believing they will anyway.***

How To Know Someone Is Here To Stay

You don't. There is no test, there is no gauge, and there is no formula that can predict whether someone stays in your life forever. You can look and see if your zodiac signs are compatible, you can compare love languages, you can sign marriage licenses and say your vows in front of a hundred people. You can get matching tattoos, you can cross pinkies, you can make pact after pact after pact, but none of this can truly guarantee that a relationship will last. **But you can hope it does.** You can hope they stay. You can hope you want to stick around, too. Because if you really think about it, love is simply a commitment to continue hoping. To continue doing your best. To continue forgiving. To continue laughing. To continue staying. So yes, nothing is certain, and sometimes this fact aches. But forever shouldn't be the goal in loving anyway. It should just be to love. And to hope.

Breaths Of Fresh Air

Souls you just instantly "click" with. Someone you've just met you didn't realize you had been missing. Humans who are endlessly kind, even to those who have been unkind to them. Friends who can correct you without being high and mighty about it. Friends who text the way they talk. Friends who get pissed off on your behalf. Those who are both proud and humble. Those who are quick to smile, to laugh, to help. Trader Joe's cashiers (you know it's true). Fair-minded folks. Gentle teachers. People who don't gossip as a means of connection. More-the-merrier planners. People who keep stepping forward, despite shaking knees. People who calm your racing heartbeat.

How To Be A Friend

Understand that to have a friend, you must *be* a friend. Show up when it matters. Give space when it's needed. Trust them to handle their own life. Accept that you don't always know what's best for them. Offer your advice when asked. Set boundaries (and stick to them). Respect their *limitations*. Reminisce. Rally. Relax. Listen to their stories, *especially* the ones you've already heard before; hear them again and again and again like it's the first time. Lend them your books. Lend them a hand. Lend them your ears. Sing in the car with the windows rolled down. Give them the benefit of the doubt. Be kind. Be there. Be patient. Ask for their opinions (even if you don't always agree). Stop trying to fix their problems. Joke around. Hold space for their feelings. Tell them when they hurt you. Listen when you wound them. Apologize. Communicate. Heal. Feel lucky. Express gratitude. See the best in them. Have difficult discussions. Have fun. Have heart. ***Hope for the best.***

THEORIES THAT EXPLAIN
WHY WE FALL IN LOVE

Because of chemistry. Because of fear. Because we missed the first bus. Because we took the elevator instead of the stairs. Because he wanted to have the family he didn't have growing up, and she craved to feel like she belonged somewhere for once. Because 2 AM is awfully heavy to handle all on your own. Because they had diluted Coca-Cola eyes. Because life is boring. Because they were the only other person at the bar on a Wednesday afternoon. Because trembling hands need something stable to hold. Because the stars aligned. Because constantly running is exhausting. Because they sat next to you in your sixth-grade history class. Because life before you learned their name was miserable. Because you got lucky. Because of the kids. Because we need hope. Because Frida wanted to be an artist. Because Springsteen wanted to write songs that reached beyond Asbury Park. Because Patti was looking for a best friend. Because we had the bravery to try. Because we wanted to believe in something bigger than ourselves. Because he gave the mousy girl a chance. Because he reminded him of the man he was too afraid to hold. Because we don't always have a choice. ***Because falling in love is what we were made as humans to do.***

THEORIES THAT EXPLAIN WHY WE FALL OUT OF LOVE

Because of mismatched fates. Because it felt too good to be true. Because of self-sabotage. Because they weren't who you thought they were. Because you weren't who they thought you were. Because of resentment. Because of fear. Because of jealousy. Because of different timezones. Because they stopped trying. Because she stopped caring. Because he stopped calling. Because two hearts are hard to wrangle. Because of loneliness. Because beautiful things are usually the most fragile. Because life is messy. Because of dishonesty. Because of pride. Because of boredom. Because people change their minds. Because of incompatibility. Because we missed the train. Because we chose ourselves. Because you deserved better. Because he wasn't listening. Because she didn't think she deserved her. Because love songs end. Because we wanted different things. Because shit got too real too fast. Because of bad timing. Because the clock struck midnight. Because of reality. Because of denial. Because we don't always have a choice. Because not all love is made to grow. Because of faith. Because of kindness. Because we have someone else to meet. Because they have someone else to meet, too. ***Because we still have hope to love again.***

An 11-Step Guide To Difficult Conversations

Step 1: Breathe in.

Step 2: Breathe out.

Step 3: Go in with the goal of resolution (not being right).

Step 4: Say what you need to say.

Step 5: Hear what the other person has to say.

Step 6: Hold space for yourself.

Step 7: Hold space for the other person.

Step 8: Take a second to recover.

Step 9: Forgive.

Step 10: Hope for the best.

Step 11: Let it go.

A List Of People Always Worth Loving

Your childhood best friend, even if you've long lost touch. The ones who make your humanity feel less heavy. The person who inspires you to do better. The person who inspires you to be kinder. The person who inspires you to dream bigger. The stranger you met in passing that you never forgot. Your college roommates who helped you become who you are today. Loyal friends. Patient listeners. Gentle speakers. Your eight-year-old self. The people you call family (blood or otherwise). Hope seekers. Those who stayed. Those who left. The ex who showed you how to love. The former best friend who taught you the importance of perspective. Your high school German teacher who believed in you when you didn't believe in yourself. The curious. The spritely. The sincere. ***Anyone who touched your soul in some way, who invited it out and allowed it to exist as all that it is, was, and will be.***

A REMINDER FOR LOVING #1

Never regret loving someone with everything you had, even if it didn't last. Even if you no longer have their number saved or if you can't remember whether their birthday was the sixth or the fifth of October or if you wouldn't *dare* say hi to them if you saw them at the bar on a Friday night. Because love is always a worthy endeavor, and no time spent loving another person is ever wasted.

Alternate Definitions For Love

Love is a hummingbird. Love is a table for one. Love is an inhale and exhale and holding your breath. Love is an undercurrent of hope. Love is chemistry. Love is commitment. Love is walking away. Love is forgetting. Love is forgiveness. Love is holding space. Love is ephemeral. Love is giving up your need to always be right. Love is a surrender. Love is an embrace. Love is a quiet and lonely affair. Love is a wakeup call. Love is a call to action. Love is not needing to say a word at all. Love is feeling brave enough to finally speak the language of your heart. Love is who would call you at 2 AM. Love is who you would answer the phone for at 2 AM. Love is running into a hug. Love is a second chance. Love is tenderness. Love is knowing glances. Love is shifting hues. Love is steady. Love is healing. Love is purpose. Love is intention. ***Love is here if you want it.***

Signs You've Found Your Platonic Soulmate

You just *know* you would have been best friends if you met when you were little kids. You've said the phrase, "We should definitely start a podcast," out loud. You sincerely believe people would listen to said podcast if you two actually pursued it. You can enjoy comfortable silences together. They're someone you trust to hold your joy. They're someone you trust to watch your dog. They're someone you trust to help you navigate the aftermath of a broken heart. You feel fiercely protective of one another. You recognize their eyes from a past life. You can give them The Look at a party if someone is being sketchy, and they'll know exactly what you're saying. They see right through you when you say, "I'm fine!" You basically have the same TikTok algorithm. They're one of the first people you want to share your good news with. And your shitty news. And your boring news. Errands are more fun when they're riding shotgun. You can laugh after a fight. They're your outfit approver, text ghostwriter, and hype person. You can talk about the heavy things and the lighter things in a single conversation. ***Time passes, things change, but your love for each other only grows stronger.***

A REMINDER FOR LOVING #2

If you're going to truly love someone, you **must** take them as all that they are. Even the pieces you don't necessarily understand or maybe even like all that much. You must stop projecting ideas about who or what, or where they should be. **This is not up to you.** Rather, you must meet them where they are at. *Wherever* that may be. You need to stand with them in everything they are and stop resenting them for everything they are not and will never be. If you're going to truly love someone, you need to love *them*. Not an idea. Not a portrait. *Them*.

Alternate Definitions For Family

Family is crimson. Family is mismatched. Family consists of those beings you can go for months without speaking to, but nothing changes. Family is chosen. Family is who you are given. Family just sort of happens. Family sees you as all that you are and still loves you anyway. Family is broken. Family is healing. Family is a phantom limb. Family your dog. Family is fate. Family is messy. Family is understanding. Family is the friend who became the sister you never had. Family is the person you start over with. Family is a sense that you've finally found belonging in the ribcages of other people. Family is a safe place. ***Family is knowing you're home for good.***

Types Of People To Hold On To, Part 3

Platonic soulmates. Read-together-in-silence friends. The person you feel safe to ugly cry in front of. The person you feel safe falling asleep next to. The person you feel safe being your full, messy self around. Your chosen family. "Let's take a walk," pals. Over-active listeners. People who aren't afraid to love openly, even if there are no guarantees. People who aren't afraid to tell the truth, even if it makes them look bad. People who aren't afraid to stand up for what's right, even if it makes them less liked. Someone who invites your inner child out to play. Anyone who you'd run through the airport for. Anyone who would run through the airport for you. The hopeful. The endlessly kind. The goofy-hearted. Beautiful minds. Gentle souls. People who inspire you to dream bigger. People who remind you that you're not alone. ***Hold them close, love them hard.***

Specific People To Look Forward To Meeting

A best friend you don't meet until you're in your 50s. A passerby who changes your perspective on the cards you've been dealt. A date you never see again but who introduces you to your favorite book. The love of your life. Your future puppy. Your future kid. Your future family. Your 40-year-old self. Your healed self. Your most authentic self. ***Anyone you didn't realize you had been missing until they walked into your life.***

Life Lessons From A Shorkie

Pause when you're happy. Walk to enjoy the world around you, not just to get from Point A to Point B. Take in the scent of flowers, good food, your favorite person. Embrace the wind. Listen for the echoes of the traffic. Believe in the good of people. Show gratitude. Be curious. Be gentle. Be goofy. Embrace the morning light. Take plenty of afternoon naps. Remember that a ride in the car always helps. Look out the window whenever you get a chance. Speak up for what you want. Keep moving. Keep playing. Keep loving.

A REMINDER FOR LOVING #3

Love is about seeing
someone's scars and
remembering you
have them too.

25 Underrated Green Flags We Need To Value More

The person who apologizes without being prompted to do so.

People who don't pretend to know more than they do, who ask questions without giving in to the fear of looking "stupid."

Someone who can answer the "stupid" questions without being condescending about it.

Friends who understand that honesty doesn't need to be delivered brutally in order to be effective.

Gentle hearts.

Enthusiastic humbleness.

Hand-talkers.

Easy listeners.

Someone who does the right thing quietly.

Folks who give compliments freely whenever they see an opportunity to.

Anyone who can teach you something new.

Jokers who get that they can be funny without being mean.

The gratefully observant. The pal who lets you know when you screwed up without shaming you in the process.

The date who holds the door (all genders applicable here).

The boss who treats you like a fellow human.

The coworker who is always offering a helping hand.

The stranger at the grocery store who smiles at whomever they happen to make eye contact with.

Moms who don't pressure you to be perfect.

Dads who make an effort to know you.

Someone who talks to kids with interest, respect, and curiosity, who remembers what it was like to be small and scared and not taken seriously.

Friends who stay later to help you clean up after you host.

The new acquaintance who asks, "What can I bring?"

The person who sends you music they think you'd love.

Anyone who feels safe, who makes you realize you're not in this life alone.

The Type Of Love You Need To Hang On To

Hang on to the type of love who feels like both an inhale and an exhale, a safe haven and an adventure. Hang on to the type of love who helps you find the words hiding beneath the tip of your tongue and the ground at your feet and a deeper meaning to your humanity. Hang on to the type of love who doesn't want to "fix" you or change you or make you wish you could fill in the outline they had of you in their mind. Hang on to the type of love who takes you as all that you are but still encourages you to become all that you can be. Hang on to the type of love who you want to run to with your good news and your bad news and your you-will-not-believe-what-happened-at-the-office-today news. Hang on to the type of love who sees the best in you even when you can't see it yourself. Hang on to the type of love who feels like home, like grace, like the person you didn't know you had been missing until they walked into your life. Invite them to stay, offer them your hand, and hope they hold on to you, too.

How To Find Your People

Let go of those who have already
let go of you. See who remains.

Just Some Voicemails I Never Got
The Chance To Leave

"You're doing better than you think you are. But you also need to take responsibility for your life. You're not hopeless. You're not helpless. You've just forgotten your power."

"I miss you. I wish I had more time with you. I sometimes still have a weird urge to call you even though you're no longer here. Muscle memory of the heart is a peculiar thing. Maybe I'll tell the sky what I need to say to you instead. I hope the clouds pass on the message."

"You hurt me. And I forgive you. But most importantly, I forgive myself."

"I'm so sorry."

"I wish you gave me another chance."

"I should have spent more time with you."

A List Of Forgotten Love Languages

"Text me when you get home." Burned CDs. Forgiveness. "*Jinx!*" Handwritten letters sent by mail. Lazy Sunday mornings. Telling the full, messy truth. Memorizing your partner's coffee order and the notes of their laugh. Running Saturday afternoon errands with your best friend. Keeping your word. Keeping a promise. Keeping your heart open. "Did you take your meds?" Hugs from behind. Surprise visits. Patience. Dancing on the front porch. "God, I'm *so* glad you're here." Surprising your mom with a clean kitchen. Saving every birthday card from the people you love. Saving your shy friend a seat at the party. Saving room for mistakes. Reading your dad's book recommendations. Telling secrets at 2 AM. Watching your roommate's favorite show with them because they love it so much. Talking about loved ones who have passed on. Night drives with the windows rolled down and music from high school turned up. "I believe in you." Giving the benefit of the doubt. Giving your full attention. Giving your full heart.

A REMINDER FOR LOVING #4

Leave people even a **little** bit more loved than you found them.

A REMINDER FOR LOVING #5

Some people are meant to love us. Others are meant to teach us. And then there are those beings who are somehow able to do a little bit of both. Cherish them all. Love them all.

THE MOMENTS
YOU HAVE TO
HOLD ON TO

The Quietest Signs Of Passing Time

Wrinkles. Age spots. Tan lines. Callused souls. Crimson ravines along your stomach. Crinkled eyes. Twilight. Lost memories. October leaves. Lukewarm coffee. The sunrise in an ever-shapeshifting sky. Dusty bookshelves. Healed wounds. Disinterested glances. Dropping temperatures. Sunburned shoulders. The pool closing at the end of summer. Sleepy bones. Faded jeans. Broken promises. Threads of gray. Missing the bus. Melting ice. Expiration dates. How it's suddenly Christmas even though you could have sworn last month was August. Timestamps from unanswered texts. Funerals for the people you loved since you were young. Remembering it's someone's birthday you lost touch with years ago. Realizing you're unsure what year that was. The end of a song. The end of an era. The end of a relationship. Low tides. Stale feelings. Regret. Scars. Waking up one day and realizing you're not who you used to be. Seeing someone you used to love but now not feeling a thing. ***When friends become strangers. When strangers become soulmates.***

When The Positive Affirmations Aren't Working...

Go for a long, meandering walk. Leave the headphones and cell at home. Be truly alone with your thoughts, no matter how much they scare you. Stop putting so much meaning into everything you think. Sit with your emotions. Lean into the pain. Feel it all, and feel it deeply. Choose forgiveness, especially when it comes to forgiving yourself. Give up perfectionism. Accept your humanity. Laugh at your mistakes. Learn from your downfalls if you can't be amused by them just yet. Ask a friend how they're really doing. Journal. Keep going for your younger self. Prove your shitty art teacher from sophomore year of high school wrong, and continue creating your artwork. Make small talk with a stranger. Remember how far you've come. Show up as who you wish you were. Be gentle with your heart. Remember, perspective and self-love take work. Believe in a better tomorrow, even if today fucking sucks. ***If you can't believe in it, hope for it.***

Some Other Types Of Gravity

Seeing someone's true colors after repainting them for years. Remembering where you came from. Remembering the shame of third grade. Remembering why you started. A second chance you don't really deserve but are grateful to be given. Your dog greeting you. "*I love you, but not in that way.*" That ever-humbling "*Oh, shit!*" moment of realizing you were the one who was in the wrong. Hearing "*not yet.*" Someone beating you to the punch. Understanding the beauty of impermanence. Coming to terms with the fact you are also made of impermanence. Contemplating what you want to do with all of that impermanence. Figuring it out.

How To Get Through A Shitty Day

Greet the aching like an old friend and truly hear what the pain has to say. Pay attention. Remember, you can't heal what you don't acknowledge even stings. Feel the bruising. Sit within the tenderness. Describe the hurt, even if it's in a language only you can understand. Call it what it is. Name your heaviness, your despair, your stolen hope. Begin to unravel that weight, that sinking feeling, that hollow faith by allowing it all to exist exactly as you feel it. Slowly learn to live with the haunting. Realize everyone has ghost stories that keep them awake at night. Talk about yours with loved ones. Listen to theirs. Laugh as you discover you were never as alone as you thought you were. See glimmers of your robbed convictions. Realize that maybe you'll never be who you used to be, that sometimes this life takes the best of you, and there's nothing you can do about that fact but build anew. Start your blueprints for constructing a better tomorrow. Feel uncertain you can even create something beautiful. ***Try like hell to do so anyway.***

Underrated Spiritual Experiences

Putting your car in park *just* as the song ends. Being seen by someone you love. Finally realizing you deserve better from yourself. Peering through stained glass windows. The moment you realize you're living in the way younger you would have wanted. When it finally stops pouring and you're able to enjoy an August afternoon. Running into a childhood friend at the bar and it's like nothing has changed, even after so many years apart. Realizing so many things haven't shifted all too much. Finding comfort in this fact.

SOME THINGS THAT PROBABLY WON'T MATTER IN THE END

Failing a final during junior year of college. The way your thighs took up a little more space than you may have liked. All the people who never bothered to learn your name. The people who never cared to understand your story. The people who couldn't love you back. How "cool" you were in high school. How "cool" you were in general. Your first job. Your first love. Your worst heartbreak. The lives you didn't live. The in-between days you don't remember now. Your worst day. Your best day.

AND SOME THINGS THAT MIGHT

How kind you were to the people who could do nothing for you. How much you cared; how much you allowed yourself to care. Who you were most days. Your willingness to forgive those who never apologized. Whether you allowed those who hurt you to color all of your future relationships. Your ability to learn from your mistakes. Your ability to admit to your mistakes. How well you said, "Sorry." Your faith in tomorrow. Your awareness of today. Your allowance of the past. How loudly you laughed. The way you spoke to yourself. The way you spoke to others. Who you were when no one was watching. How deeply you loved.

Signs Of A Life Being Fully Lived

Coffee-stained teeth. Baggy eyes. Skinned seven-year-old knees. Sore muscles. A heavy heart. Stretch marks. Little ravines at the outer corners of your eyes. Laugh lines. A red wine splotch on the brand-new couch. Smeared lipstick. Stumbling into love. Getting dumped. Baby announcements from childhood pals. Calloused heels. Eye contact. Snort laughs. Bewilderment. Anger. Jealousy. Nostalgia. Disappointment. Dancing badly at weddings. Daydreaming. Making mistakes. A damn good cry. A vodka-drenched kitchen to clean after hosting your best friends the previous evening. Attending funerals of the people you'll always love. Mascara marks you can't get out of the pillowcase. Forgetting to check your phone. 3 AM makeouts. Regret. Bitterness. Sadness. Joy. Seeing your parents as the imperfect humans they are and loving them more for it. Awkward silences. Giggling as you leave the hot server your number. Craving alone time. Disagreements. Sheer delight. Getting lost in a book. Losing your way on a road trip. Getting home later than you wanted to because you didn't feel the time pass. Bygone conversations with Lyft drivers, grocery store clerks, the mail lady. Forgiveness. Letting go of the things that aren't meant for you. ***Understanding you'll never have all the answers, but continuing to ask the questions anyway.***

20 Reasons To Look Up From Your Phone

Because the clouds are taking a vacation
Because it's 75 degrees and you're sitting inside on the couch
Because there are books to be read
Because your own story needs to be told
Because there's music to be blasted with your windows open
Because your friend deserves your undivided attention
Because what you see online is not always the truth
Because comparison is a bitch
Because you're missing out on the laughter
Because you haven't finished your painting
Because you haven't finished your sentence
Because you haven't finished watching the movie
Because you're missing out on the moment in front of you
Because there are hands to be held
Because there are more interesting things to look at
Because your dog wants you
Because there are better ways to waste your time
Because the email can wait
Because the text can wait
Because your life cannot wait

A REMINDER FOR LIVING #1

Notice the moments that
make you forget your phone.
Who are you with?
What are you doing?
How are you feeling?
Do more of that.

How To The Trust The Good Things When They Come Along

Take a minute. And another. And then another. Step out of your body and observe yourself from a stranger's perspective. Pretend you don't know your haunting, your darkness, your worst thoughts. Imagine what you would feel if you stopped referencing the past as evidence that nothing ever works out. Remind yourself that you're worthy of the good things, too. Reframe your thoughts from, "I can't believe this will last" to "I am so damn lucky this is happening." Make way for awe. Make room for hope. Make space for the present. Stop mining for reasons why it will never work. Stop looking backward and for the writing on the wall and look at it head-on instead. Hold the fear and the faith all at once. Accept your lack of control. Remind yourself you can always pick up the shoe if it drops. In the meantime, be willing to welcome the lightness of something aligning. Lean in. Redefine what trust means. Remember that being negative doesn't make you deeper. It only makes you hurt.

Just A List Of Potential Blessings In Disguise

Not getting invited to the party. Being stood up by your Hinge date. Losing the promotion. Getting dumped. Getting ghosted. Getting left on read. Hearing "not yet." Learning something the hard way. Taking a wrong turn. Sleeping past your alarm. Forgetting your phone at home. Missing the joke. Missing the first bus. Missing the person you used to be. Seeing someone's true colors before you're ready to. Realizing you have to let them go, even though it hurts. Falling in love later in life. Falling for the "wrong person." Falling out with a friend. Moving back home. Going through the motions for three weeks straight. Running late. Growing pains. "Bad timing." Calling three people to hang out on a Friday night and only getting their voicemails. Having to initiate a difficult conversation. Anything beautiful ending. Grief. Heartbreak. Closure. Anger. Waiting. Longing. Disappointment. Regret. Fear. ***Because these are all second chances, and I hope you come to see them in this way. But mostly, I hope you take them. I really hope you do.***

Some Very Specific Things To Look Forward To

The mornings you don't have to set your alarm and can wake up when your body *actually* feels like it. Hugging your best friend after a year of not seeing them. A full-body cry. First kisses. Last days of work before a vacation. Unhinged nights that make you feel alive. Making a toast at your best friend's wedding. Saying your vows to the love of your life. Breaking up with the person who is no good for you. A cool shower after an insanely sweaty workout. The first sip of coffee in the morning tomorrow. Coney island scrambled eggs. Rihanna's new album. Overcoming something you thought you never would. Laughing so hard your stomach hurts. Your favorite song to be released in 2024. Your favorite show to come out in 2033. Deep appreciation. Awe. Dangerous eye contact with your crush at a party. When the lights dim at a concert, and a rush goes through the crowd. Realizing you didn't wake up thinking of the person who broke your heart for the first time in six weeks. The plane landing. Walking in the door to your dog after a trip. Self-pride. Getting your eyeliner *just* right on the first try. Truffle fries. Meeting someone you didn't know you had been missing. Realizing you have the things younger you would have wanted. The moment of recognition that this is your one life and thinking, ***"Finally. This is it. This is mine."***

An Incomplete List Of Things You (Probably) Won't Regret

Doing the right (but difficult) thing. Saying what you truly feel, not what you think makes you look more composed or better. Taking a chance on love. Taking your power back. Taking your joy seriously. Asking for help when you need it. Understanding that focusing on what-is is far better than living with what-ifs. Being honest when someone hurts you. Standing up for the underdog. Apologizing even if someone won't forgive you. Telling someone you love them even if they don't love you back. Just fucking going for something you *really* want, even if that something might not work out. Allowing room for dessert. Allowing someone to dislike you without trying to convince them otherwise. Allowing yourself to be human.

AN OBSERVATION

You will probably find you regret more of the things you **didn't** do than the mistakes you made.

A Series Of Moments That Can Change Your Life (Part 1)

"I want to break up." Getting the job offer. Moving somewhere new by yourself. A split-second decision on the highway. "Will you marry me?" Signing the adoption papers for the dog you've always wanted. Unlocking the door to the first apartment you'll rent all on your own. The last sentences of a novel. "We got your biopsy results..." Filling out an intake form for therapy. Clicking "send" on the risky text. Feeling utterly alone in a crowded room. A missed call. An epiphany. A mistake. "It's not your fault." Going on the random Thursday afternoon Hinge date. Leaving the party early. Staying out for one more drink. Blocking their number. Choosing compassion. Choosing the truth, even when it hurts. Choosing yourself.

A Series Of Turning Points

Breaking up with the person you love but have outgrown. Changing careers. Changing your mind. Changing your bedding. Spending more time alone. Staying in your lane. Taking a break from a vice. Giving up your need for control. Giving in to joy. Giving Harry Styles another chance. Swiping right on a dating app. Blocking their number (you know the one). Accountability. Forgiveness. Gratitude. Asking for guidance. Sending the risky text. Signing up for therapy. Boundaries. Heartbreak. Rearranging your furniture. Speaking your mind. Standing your ground. Admitting your mistakes. Rejection. Remorse. Regret. Turning off your notifications. Finishing a book that changes your perspective on everything. Letting yourself really cry. Doing something for someone else for no other reason than to be kind. Walking the middle path. Walking a new way home. Walking away from the things that no longer serve you. Remembering that hurt people hurt people but healed people heal people, too. Trusting the good things when they come along. Letting them be on their way when it's time.

WHAT YOU MISS WHILE YOU'RE WAITING FOR THE OTHER SHOE TO DROP

The moment slipping
through your fingers.

You're Allowed To Just Live, Too

You don't have to understand everything in order to experience it. Not everything needs deep analysis. Because honestly, some shit just isn't that deep. You don't need to interpret why something makes you feel joy or sadness or fear. You just need to feel it. You need to let it in, let it be, and then let it be on its way.

A List Of Things Always Worth Chasing

Joy. Awe. Purpose. That inkling you could be doing something more with your life. Kindness. Compassion. The word teasing the tip of your tongue that would **perfectly** describe how you're feeling. The day dancing in front of you. Saturday night shenanigans. A better tomorrow. Play. Platonic soulmates. Places that remind you of home. The little things and the grand things, too. Burning desire. Ideas so fucking absurd they *just* might work. The naked truth. The bigger picture. Dreams. Curiosity. Pride. Your healing. Your balance. Your intuition. That rush the bridge of your favorite song gives you. Dogs. Prickling anger. Drunken despair. A full-body laugh. Crushes, even if they might not work out. Difficult but necessary lessons. Good conversation. Humbleness. The last train out of the city. The first cup of coffee in the morning. Budding strength. Hopeful quiet. Depth. Lightness. The middle path. New perspectives. Mindset shifts. Accountability. Forgiveness. Trust. The sunrise. The full moon. Your north star. The cloudless sky. 4 AM questions. 5 AM epiphanies. Faith. Yourself. Your work. Your art. Your family, chosen or otherwise. Something to believe in. Someone to fight for. *Anything that makes you feel glad to exist right here, right now.*

A REMINDER FOR LIVING #2

Life isn't meant to be figured out.
It's meant to be experienced.

Moments That Prove You're Healing (Even If You Don't See It Just Yet)

Realizing the way you'd react now is not the same way you would have last year. Looking back on something that hurt you with a neutral mindset. Looking back on someone who hurt you with fondness. Looking back at a situation that used to confuse you with pristine clarity. Fully grasping a silly moment without feeling the need to justify it. Asking for help. Having the bandwidth to lend a hand. Forgiving (yourself *and* others). Giving yourself the benefit of the doubt. Trusting your decision and not asking every person you know if it's the right one. No longer fearing sadness and anger and jealousy and contempt. Walking through your days with a *consistent* feeling of contentment and peace. Allowing the darkness lingering at the doorway of your being and the lightness dancing on the edges of your feet to coexist.

Just Some Things That Take Courage

Falling in love. Falling *out* of love. Existing freely in a body that the world wants you to hate. Telling someone they upset you. Signing up for therapy. Taking a new job. Quitting a toxic job. Setting a boundary with someone you love. Sending the risky text. Detaching from the outcome. Showing up on the days you want to stay under the covers. Saying no. Saying yes. Hope. Acknowledging you were wrong. Facing the parts of yourself you want to hide away. Going to the party even though you'll see your ex for the first time since the breakup. Moving somewhere new on your own. Allowing yourself to be seen as you are, not as who you are pretending to be. Wearing what you want to wear, not what you *think* you should wear. Believing in something even though life has shown you every other reason not to. Being disliked. Asking for help. Trusting your gut. Forgiving the person who hurt you the most, even if that person is yourself. Sewing your patchwork heart onto your wrist for all to see. Explaining the full, ugly, and messy truth. Remembering you know nothing. Singing. Dancing. Playing. Leaning into sadness. Learning a new language. Trying. Expressing disappointment. Embracing unbridled joy. Making room for uncertainty. Letting go of the past. Giving yourself the chance you wish others gave you. Hoping for the best. ***Continuing to stand back up, no matter how many times you get knocked down.***

BEFORE A MOMENT
BECOMES A MEMORY...

Hold it close.

A Series Of Moments That Can Change Your Life (Part 2)

Filing for divorce even when it kills you because you know that staying would be far worse. Being the first member of your family to attend college. Getting laid off from the job you thought you'd retire from on your own terms. An abrupt knock on your door at 3 AM. "Can we talk in private?" Forgetting an important deadline. The final sip of the last drink you realize you will ever let yourself have. Being left on read by someone you thought would be in your life forever. An apology, given or received. Saying a prayer for the first time in years because you don't feel like you have anyone else to talk to. Picking up a paintbrush. Buying a one-way plane ticket and never looking back. Accepting your family for who they are. Another negative pregnancy test after months and months of trying. Taking a chance on grace. Taking a chance on talking to a cute stranger at the bar. Taking a chance on yourself.

A List Of Underrated Art Forms

Apologizing. Making friends in adulthood. Remembering someone's name after a *single* mention. A well-timed pun. Somehow arriving on time despite running late. Letting go of the things that no longer serve you. Friendship breakups. Accepting a compliment without going inward or deflecting. Being funny without being mean. Being kind without being a doormat. Being yourself without caring what anyone else thinks about you. The spontaneous phone call. Handwritten letters. Cursive. Journalism. Learning a new language. Stumbling through anxiety. Navigating awkward silences without ending the conversation. Compassion. Distinguishing your fear from your intuition. Translating a two-year-old's sentences. Rebuilding a life. Rebuilding a family. Rebuilding a home. Metaphors. Planning a date. Learning to drive. Taking responsibility for your life. ***Helping heal a heart you didn't break, especially when that heart is your own.***

Pay attention to...

The wind. The bare night sky. The choreography of your heartbeat. What makes your eyes light up. How someone makes you feel after you're with them. Moments that make your shoulders tense up. Moments that make your anxiety go a little more quiet. Moments that make you feel utterly and stupidly alive. The book you're reading. The notes of the song you're listening to. The way a friend reacts when you tell them that they hurt you. Apologies without changed behavior. Your intuition. Your anger. Your hurt. Your healing. Good manners. Expectations. Boundaries. The road ahead of you. Who makes you feel safe. Who makes you feel uneasy. Who makes you feel understood. Your best friend sharing their ghost stories with you. Who celebrates your wins. Little kids. Your tone. Your words. Your inner child. Your soul's calling. The things that stir your curiosity. The things that paint goosebumps along your arms. The things that invite your hope to come out of hiding. Whatever you're feeling right here, right now. ***Your life.***

THE FEELINGS
YOU HAVE TO
HOLD ON TO

SOME THINGS HEARTBREAK IS
(AND SOME THINGS IT IS NOT)

Heartbreak is...

Painful. Unavoidable. Frustrating. A damn nuisance. Humbling. Distracting. Another chance. A blessing in disguise. Inspiring. All-encompassing. A sign of life. A muse. Proof you tried. Proof you cared. Proof you loved. Bravery. Human. *A new beginning.*

Heartbreak is not...

Enjoyable. Avoidable. Forever. An indictment of your character. An indictment of *their* character. A failure. A sign you are unlovable. Something you cannot get through. Something you can ignore. A place to stay. *The end.*

The softness of…

The end of September. Rose-colored beginnings. The edges of Lake Michigan's waves. Stained glass. Smudged kohl eyeliner. Gentle nudges forward. Cashmere apologies. Forgiveness. Pinky promises. Whispered compliments. "You're enough just as you are." The Lyft ride home at the end of a late night out. Feeling alone in a crowded room. Falling asleep. Falling in love. Falling leaves. Giving a hesitant smile after a disagreement with your partner. Baby tummies. Monet paintings. Aching bones. Bruised egos. Understanding. Compassion. Trust. Waking up slowly. A Sunday without plans. "I'm not going anywhere." The last drops of rain after an unexpected storm. Regina Spektor melodies. Fading memories. Fading tattoos. Fading resentment. Goosebumps. Streetlights reflected in puddles. Fireflies stopping by to say hello in the summer. Wishing you could freeze a moment in time. Wishing you could bottle up the sound of your favorite person's laugh and save it for later. Wishing you could fly. The fact you cannot do any of these things. A string of Christmas lights. The way hope tends to linger, even when everything feels hopeless. ***Realizing that's how faith works.***

Some Underrated Forms Of Magic

Heartbreak. Nostalgia. Love. Intuition. Someone texting you *just* as you were thinking about them. Running late for work but managing to hit every green light on the drive in so you still show up on time anyway. Finding the word dancing on the tip of your best friend's tongue. Feeling at home in someone else's arms. Actually falling asleep soon after your head hits the pillow. Finally letting go of someone who is no good for you. Clicking with someone new. Meeting someone you didn't know you had been missing. Strokes of genius. Art. A baby drifting to sleep on your shoulder. Writing and using a word you didn't even realize that you knew. Forgiveness. Inside jokes. A dog's love. Foreshadowing. A surprise album from your favorite artist. Unfounded faith that ends up seeing itself through. Fixing a friendship you thought was broken beyond repair. Hope in the midst of despair. Being here despite it all. **Staying because you want to see what happens next.**

Glimmers Of Hope

Tiny libraries. Baroque paintings. Science fairs. September. The last day of school before summer vacation. The first notes of "Robbers" by The 1975. Second chances. Daily to-do lists. Pinky promises. Good intentions. Random acts of kindness. Planning a trip with your best friends a year in advance. Changing lanes. Changing the channel. Changing your surroundings. Throwing loose change in a jar labeled "Chicago." Going out on a first date. Agreeing to a second date. Lending your favorite book. Smiling at a cute stranger across the dive bar. Flirting with reckless abandon. "Will you marry me?" Adopting the dog you've always wanted. Wilted spinach. Whispered secrets. Texting first. Apologizing first. Showing up to the party first. Making New Year's Resolutions. "Okay, I'll stay for one more drink." Poetry. Cardinals. Signing up for therapy. Believing in a higher power. Planting a garden. Trying something again. Having the inkling your life is about to change for the better. Treating this feeling as truth even though you have no tangible reason to. ***Not needing one.***

There is space for both...

Forgiveness *and* accountability. Love *and* boundaries. Self-respect *and* humility. Humor *and* stoicism. Compassion *and* walking away. Gentleness *and* assertiveness. Fear *and* courage. Doubt *and* faith. Kindness *and* anger. Resentment *and* gentleness. Body *and* soul. Heart *and* mind. Loss *and* gains. The past *and* the future. The ebbs *and* the flows. The high *and* low tides. The moon *and* the sun. The shadows *and* the light. Wishing *and* reality. Rejection *and* redirection. Letting go *and* remembering. Metaphors *and* saying it plain. Indulgence *and* just enough. Goodbyes *and* new beginnings.

The tenderness of…

"*Thank God, I didn't want to go out either!*" Being told the whole truth. Being told "*no.*" Being told off by your boss and feeling like a kid all over again. Realizing younger you deserved more grace. Feeling a lump in your throat take shape as you remember all the times you could have been kinder to little you, too. Spending Saturday night alone but not feeling lonely. Saying you're "fine" when you know you're not. Staying quiet about the aching because you don't want to be a burden. Coming to terms with the fact someone isn't the person you thought they were. Suppressed disappointment. A hug when you really needed it. Forgiving someone you thought you couldn't. Looking across the table at the person you once loved and realizing there's nothing left to say. Wishing you could find a few words anyway. Being understood instead of being judged. Accidentally brushing your hand against your crush's and being disappointed they didn't hang on. Relaxing your shoulders. Loosening your grip on your life. Letting the cards fall where they may. **Hoping for better things while tears fall down your face.**

Various Ways To Express A Feeling

"You really hurt me." Sketching in charcoal. Crying in the shower. Running without a destination in mind. Screaming into your pillow. Writing it down. *"I'm so glad you exist at the same time as me."* Singing in the car alone because only you and Linkin Park understand what you're going through. Yoga flows. Nurturing the leftover love you have for someone who passed on. Dancing and letting the music guide your limbs. Letting out a sigh. *"I wanted it to be you so bad."* Love notes. Goodbye letters you'll never send. Volunteering for a cause you care deeply about. Letting whatever you feel wash over you with grace, with acceptance, with fullness.

Things That Feel Like Therapy That Aren't Technically Therapy

Driving with your windows rolled all the way down while scream-singing music from high school on a two-lane freeway. Saying how you *really* feel, not just saying what you *think* you should be feeling. Crying it out. Sweating it out. Someone hearing you out. When your dog is so incredibly grateful you came home despite the fact you always do and always will. Typing out *the* paragraph text to someone you're sort of dating who has been treating you like shit. Deleting it and remembering you deserve better instead. Acting like you deserve better. Notes app poetry you'll never share but are happy you wrote anyway because it was just for you. Calling your best friend. Sex with someone who loves you. The thrill of going out for a night and being someone else for a little while. Dancing until 2 AM. Falling asleep as soon as your head hits the pillow. Actually sleeping through the night. Waking up feeling brand new.

Sadness is…

Heaviness. Softness. Tenderness. 2 o'clock on Monday morning when you can't sleep because your bed feels too big for its own good. Demanding. Lingering. Distracting. Being left on read after spilling your heart. Honest. Humbling. Human.

Happiness is…

Perennial. A vacation home in the clouds. The people who stayed. The people you let go. The people who were lessons. The songs you never get sick of listening to. Re-reading an old favorite. Side-splitting laughter. A hug when you *really* need it. Unexpected grace. Gentleness. Sometimes a slow burn. Sometimes just a moment. Sometimes merely passing through.

How To Stop Overthinking Fucking Everything

Take a deep breath. Hold it. Count to five. Exhale. Repeat as often as necessary. Talk it out. Take a break. Take a walk. Take some time for yourself. Ask for help. Remember that no one is thinking about you as much as you are thinking about you. Consider this to be a relief. Understand most things are forgivable, including you. Stop defining yourself by your mistakes and simply learn from it all instead. Stop judging other people for their shortcomings and forgive them while you're at it. Sit with the quiet. Check the facts. Check yourself. Check the front door once. Choose compassion. Remind yourself that preparing for the worst does not make you more prepared for the worst; it just makes you suffer. Trust that you can get through anything that comes your way. Trust your judgment. Trust your heart. Live from a place of hope, not fear.

Some Other Types Of Poetry

Someone being able to make you laugh even though you're in the middle of crying. Sun sneaking through the blinds early in the morning. A lingering hug. Quiet understandings. Comfortable silences. Forgetting to check your phone. Remembering you're just a speck in an ever-expanding universe. Being humbled and terrified by this fact. Unyielding effort. Meeting someone you never thought you would. Being grateful that you crossed paths, even if they diverged. Making dangerous eye contact. Talking to your dog. Telling secrets to the moon. Express gratitude. Giving a sincere apology. Crinkly eyes. Racing hearts. Rough hands. Hard work. The rush before calling your crush. The empty spaces you notice once someone has gone. A chaotic first kiss you didn't think was going to happen. A frantic last kiss you never thought would be. Tattoos. The hopeful tension you experience before holding someone's hand for the first time. The moment they fold their fingers over yours in return. Grace without explanations. Waking up not thinking about the cracks in your heart for the first time in weeks. ***Being brave enough to show up as all that you are, not just a shadow of who you wish you could be.***

An Incomplete List Of Some Of The Best Feelings

Opening the door to your warm apartment after walking in late January air. Running into a hug from your friend at the airport. Package delivery. The exhale of resolution. When your friend admits she doesn't want to go out either. When someone accepts your apology, or you hear "sorry" when you thought it would never be said. Sending the risky text and getting an even riskier reply. When the dog chooses you at the party. Meeting up with an old friend, but it's like no time has passed. Finding your keys after you had been looking for 20 minutes and were about to lose your mind. A long-awaited cry. The first sip of coffee in the morning. When you listen to a new song, and the lyrics were *exactly* what you needed to hear at that moment in time. Laughing fits. When you think of the damn word that had been dancing on the edge of your tongue. Walking to your car after an amazing first date. When your school finally called the snow day. Seeing your loved ones become all they wanted to be. Forgiveness. Drunken dancing. Comfortable silences. Finishing a book and needing to sit with it for a few minutes afterward because it was just that good. Realizing that everything you have is what younger you once wanted and knowing how proud they'd be to see you made it. That you turned out okay after all.

THE SWEETNESS OF...

Realizing you forgot to think of the person who broke your heart all day. Not feeling the desire to chase their image in your mind's eye. Mutual understanding. A quiet Friday night. Flirting with someone new. Noticing you have a crush on this person. Feeling hope they might feel the same way. A baby's laugh. A dog chasing their tail. A child comforting their friend. Watching two strangers clearly hitting it off on a first date. Personalized wedding vows. Playful teasing. Believing one little thing could change your whole life. Pursuing that little thing with the utmost hope.

THE BITTERSWEETNESS OF...

Missing someone but not wanting them back in your life. Deleting the text thread with your former situationship since you no longer need it. A kiss with someone you know will be the last you'll share together. Remembering a portion of your life as far more beautiful than it probably was. Still believing there was beauty to be found in that time period anyway. Yearning. Waiting. Hoping. Half-assing a paper in college and still getting a good grade somehow. Feeling all of the unfulfilled potential that rests in your bones, quiet and untouched. Keeping your grandparents' home phone number saved even though their house is on the verge of being sold since no one lives there anymore. Writing down the date and realizing it's the birthday of someone you no longer speak to. Justified anger. Re-reading old diary entries from a younger, more chaotic version of yourself and still seeing yourself throughout the pages. Realizing maybe old versions of ourselves never leave us. Forgetting a memory. Forgetting a feeling. Forgetting what you saw in the person sitting across from you. Realizing how good you had something you no longer have. Appreciating you got to experience the good thing anyway. Wishing you still could.

The Best Types Of Inspiration

Empty spaces. Shadows of tree branches dancing in the summer wind. Mistakes. Hard lessons. Difficult goodbyes. A damn good thunderstorm. Romantic comedies. Vintage clothes. Old magazines. 3 AM. Oil paintings. Rough hands. Curated Spotify playlists. Forgotten furniture on the side of the road. Taking the scenic route home. Dogs looking out the window. Love. Loss. Longing. Remembering why you started. Remembering what you adored as a kid. Remembering that you're still allowed to enjoy those things now. Serendipity. Grace. Hard work. Looking up from your phone. People-watching. Heartbreak. First dates. Last kisses. Final words. Deep conversations. Boredom. Asking more questions. Answering your own musings. Listening intently to what the quiet has to say. Thrift stores. Charcoal. Sketchbooks. Memoirs. Documentaries. 1960s newspapers. ***Feeling everything that you do and feeling it deeply.***

THE PIECES OF
YOURSELF YOU HAVE
TO HOLD ON TO

2

Please don't lose your…

Curiosity. Compassion. Clarity. Darkness. Lightness. Grayness. Childlike wonder. Mischief. Teenage rage. Questions. Humility. Humanity. Harmless stupidity. Peculiarity. Sundays and Wednesdays and in-between days, too. Grand gestures. Bigger pictures. Shades of blue. Love stories. Openness. Tendency to try and do the right thing. Tenderness when you get it wrong. Absurd ideas. North stars. Pivot points. Mistakes. Lessons. Courage. Ability to care deeply. Poetry. Power. Principles. Determination. Grit. Unfinished novels. Unfinished business. Unfinished healing. Vulnerability. 3 AM heart-to-hearts. Intuition. Second chances. Jagged edges. Contrasts. Soul's calling. Chaos. Manners. Fire. Honesty. Momentum. Gravity. Connection. Need to know what happens next. Desire to try again and again and again. Hope. Potential. Perspective. Purpose. Voice. Heart. Backbone. People. *Self.*

How To Love Yourself Better

Slow down when you're happy. Forget about the rush of society's deadlines. Focus on what you want instead. Practice trusting your own choices. Take accountability for those decisions, even when they don't go the way you hoped they would. Learn from your mistakes. Remember when you got it right, too. Protect your energy. Stop trying to impress people you don't even like. Ask for help. Keep learning. Keep hoping. Keep both feet on the ground. Stay close to those who feel like home. Let go of anyone who makes you question your worth. Be vulnerable. Be fair. Be open. Live according to your own values and build a life that feels like yours. Take care of your mind. Nourish your body. Feed your soul. Chase your joy. Heal. Embrace solitude. Stop apologizing for taking up space. Say what you need to say. Feel what you need to feel. Stop expecting yourself to be perfect. Allow yourself to be human. Look around you. Celebrate the little wins. Accept the downfalls with as much grace as you can muster. Forgive yourself when you fall short. ***Try again. Try again. Try again. Never stop trying.***

SELF-LOVE REMINDER #1

You don't have to be useful
in order to be loved.

Some Things I Wish I Could Tell
My 17-Year-Old Self

You don't have to explode to be noticed. You don't win that friend group over; stop trying to. People are going to talk shit; let them. You know the truth. You have sincere intentions with awkward execution (you get more skillful). I understand you, even if you feel like nobody else does. Some texts are better left unsent. You will never be "too much" for the right people. That said, you will be "too much" for others, and you need to respect that. You can laugh at yourself without making yourself the joke. Don't give up on your art. Don't give up on yourself. Don't give away your power. Slow down. Spend as much time with Granny as possible. Forgive yourself. You're really, really, really bad at math, but you're going to need to keep showing up to class anyway. Dump him. Stay curious. Keep reading. Keep burning your friends' CDs. Keep your heart on your sleeve (but maybe cover it up every now and then). You're allowed to feel things deeply but work on how you express those emotions. You become friends with your parents, cut them more slack. You finally find your people. You're not alone. You get into college. You turn into a writer. You help others. You get your shit together. You're not so bad, be kinder to yourself. ***Hang on, it gets better.***

An Incomplete List Of Signs You're Loved

"*Let me help you with that.*" The way your shoulders are sought to steady trembling lips. How you can invite laughter out to play despite your sister's tear-stained face. "*Tell me when you land.*" Happy birthday texts. Reaching hands. Pats on the back. Hugs that linger. "Will you be my bridesmaid?" Late-night chats. Being anyone's Friday night plans. Being your best friend's north star. Being your daughter's comfort person. Being the reason someone stayed out later. Your dad laughing at your puns. "*I thought you'd love this song.*" Your mom asking for your advice. The dog picking you at the party. "*I'm so proud of you.*" Your grandma leaving you voicemails. I miss you texts. Someone finishing your sentences. Sincere apologies. Benefit of the doubt. Your friend getting excited on your behalf. Grace. "*Just calling because I wanted to hear your voice.*" **The fact you exist.**

SELF-LOVE REMINDER #2

————————— You deserve to get better.

Healing is…

Appreciating autumn again. Keeping both your feet planted firmly on the ground. Admitting you're hurting. Asking for help. Offering a hand. Laughing uproariously. Accepting what you can't control and taking charge of what you can. Allowing room for grace and sleeping in on Sunday mornings and afternoon walks in the winter when the sun finally stops by to say hello. Holding yourself accountable. Spending time with the people who feel like hope. Facing yourself. Facing your haunting. Facing forward anyway. Remembering you can always try again. Trying again. And again, And again. Bleeding poetry. Stitching up the heart you intentionally ripped off your sleeve. Blasting "Chinatown" on repeat while cleaning your room for the first time in months. Seeing your therapist on the days you'd rather hide. Reminding yourself it's going to be okay. Believing what you just said. Crying your eyes out to "Scott Street." Telling shame you did the best you could with the tools you had at the time. Realizing you deserve to get better. Getting better as a result.

What I'd Tell Myself If I Were My Own Best Friend

If I were my own best friend, I'd tell myself that the pieces I want to hide away really aren't so bad. I'd tell myself that most people feel broken and incomplete and jagged and scared and fucked in the head, and this doesn't make them exempt from belonging, so why would it make me?

If I were my own best friend, I'd tell myself that my past doesn't define me, but it can teach me if I'd let it. I'd tell myself that I have made mistakes and been messy and stupid and wrong, but this just makes me human. I'd tell myself I did the best I could with the information I had, and now I know better, so I can do better, too. I'd tell myself I'm worthy of my own grace. I'd tell myself I'm worthy of my own love.

If I were my own best friend, I'd tell myself that not everything happens for a reason, but most things do have a tendency to work out okay. I'd tell myself that I am exactly where I need to be, even if it's not what I pictured for myself at 30. I'd tell myself that life is never going to be what we imagine it to be, but that's part of the magic of being here.

I'd tell myself to get out of my head and step into my life. I'd tell myself to stop thinking so much about living and just live. I'd tell myself, "*Please, just live.*"

SELF-LOVE REMINDER #3

You are allowed to outgrow the life you thought you wanted. You are under no obligation to stay in places you no longer want to be, even if those places exist only in your mind and heart. You're allowed to move on. You're allowed to evolve. You're allowed to change. You're allowed to become who you actually are.

Some Things That Don't Exclude You From Love

Your messy mind. Your haunted heart. Your misshapen moments. Your shame. Your guilt. Your pain. Your intrusive thoughts. The fact you spent most of the age of 24 hungover. How many people you've slept with. Your psych ward getaway. The echoes of your self-doubt reverberating throughout your body. Your clumsy family dynamic. Your shattered faith. The fact that you are not perfect.

Some Shit I Haven't Learned How To Do Just Yet

Sleep through the night. Leave well enough alone. Take my time. Take myself seriously. Take a chance on actually finding love. Spell "Wednesday" without thinking "Wed-NES-day" in my head. Be kinder to myself. Graceful exits. Trust the free fall. Rewrite my narrative. Use dating apps without wanting to throw my phone at the wall. Paint in watercolor. Face boredom without feeling like I'm crawling in my own skin. Be still. Be careful. Be mindful. Tame my inner angry teen. Know that maybe she was allowed to be fucking pissed. Realize that perhaps she just needed to learn to manage her rage better. Snowboard. Salsa dance. Speak with conviction about the things I know to be true. Forgive who I've been. Forgive fate. Forgive Sunday School. Algebra. Find my center of gravity. See the bigger picture. Understand I don't need to. Not yet.

How To Catch Your Breath

Stop. Be *really* still. Feel the ground cradling the bottom of your feet and trace that sensation from the very tips of your toes to the soles. Notice what that feels like, being held by the earth. Describe the pressure of gravity and be comforted by the fact that there are forces greater than you to hold you down. To keep you here. To make you stay. Look around. Realize your breathing has slowed a little and that your heartbeat has steadied a bit. Take a deep breath. Pause. Release it. Take a deep breath. Pause. Release it. Take a deep breath. Pause. Release it. ***Realize you had your breath all along; it's just about working with it, not against it.***

How To Fall Back In Love With Your Life

Acknowledge that the magic is gone. After all, you can't find what you never even admitted was missing in the first place. Retrace your steps trying to find it. Pray you'll be able to pick up right where you left off, not unlike seeing a friend you lost touch with and always missed or finally grasping that word dancing on the edges of your tongue. Figure falling back in love with your life will feel kind of like that: a reconciliation, a reunion, an epiphany.

Start seeking what you know you once loved. Look for your misplaced hope in all of those familiar spots where it used to hide. The bottom of a wine glass. Within the characters of your comfort TV shows. In the pages of your old favorite books. At happy hours with friends and during late-night chats with crushes and at the tips of your fingers as you write.

Attempt it all. Still feel hollow. Slowly begin to notice that all of those places you've been and adored seem so very different now. It's just not the same. Understand it's probably because you're no longer the same either. Contemplate what shifted. Wonder if you can ever go back to who you were. Come to terms with the fact that you can't, and maybe you don't want to after all.

Take the hint that no reunion will be planned, and no moment of clarity will be had. Accept the incompatibility of what once was with what now is. Forget trying to figure out what shifted. Understand that this is nothing but a distraction from what you must do next. Embrace the fact that sometimes what once worked no longer does and that you have no choice but to build anew.

Begin again. Start from scratch. Try to do things differently, to look at things differently, too. Redefine awe. Invite wonder to Sunday brunch with your friends and think about the fact that you're so lucky you exist during the same lifetime as them. Be thrilled that you get to have your morning cup of coffee on the front porch. Watch the sun melt into the horizon during a random June night and feel the quiet, humming hope return to your veins.

Finally, discover that magic isn't something that's found and that maybe it never really left you in the first place. Maybe loving your life is something you need to work at and keep trying to wrangle. Only when you accept that the magic you thought you were missing actually rests in your own hands will you find yourself spellbound once again.

That is how you fall back in love with your life.

Things That Are Far More Interesting About You Than Your Looks

How well you apologize (and how willingly you apologize, too). Your ability to be kind despite being pissed as *hell*. The courage you are able to muster despite the fact worst-case scenarios are running through your mind. The way you treat people who work in the service industry. The way you make people feel about themselves. The way you handle frustration. Your tenacity. What makes you laugh. What makes you cry. What makes you enraged. Your favorite song. Your scars. Your hope. Your humanity.

Read This When You Forget Your Worth

When you forget your worth, please know that you are not an afterthought. You are not an idea that needs mulling over. You are not an option. You are not second best. And anyone who makes you feel any of those ways doesn't deserve you anyway.

Growing Pains That Are Part Of Life

Looking at someone you once loved and being unable to name a damn reason why. Missing someone and not wanting them back. Reflecting on former versions of yourself and cringing. Getting ghosted by someone you trusted with your heart. Understanding your parents are human, not perfect. Realizing your parents are only getting older. Turning 28 and lamenting everything you haven't done yet. Turning 30 and noticing that not much has changed since 28. Worrying that you may never become everything you wanted to be. Coming to terms with the fact that you may have to be okay with that.

How To Save Yourself

Take a deep breath. Say what you can't hold in. Stop labeling emotions as "good" or "bad" and just let them exist as they are in all of their fucked up glory. Let yourself exist as all that you are, too. Replace shame with compassion. Take accountability for the things you've messed up. Do better next time. Forgive yourself. Forgive fate. Forgive the traffic light for turning red when you were already running late. Stop taking everything so personally. Accept what you can't control. Take matters into your own hands when you can. Blast music while you clean your room. Let go of those who have already let go of you and give yourself the chance you wish they gave you. Break down. Rebuild. Grow up. Remember that what you think is awful about you is what so many others worry about too. Remind yourself that nothing is ever as bad as you think, including you. ***Keep going. Keep trying. Keep your head up.***

Things I Regret The Most

Saying the witty but unkind thing. Caring too much about what people who don't like me think. Breaking myself trying to make those people care. Double texting that guy who I knew deep down would still leave me on read (he did). Begging to be understood by someone who already decided they didn't want to understand me. Trying too hard. Not trying enough. Not trying at all. Giving into my anger in unhealthy ways. Focusing too much on the future rather than a beautiful moment I had slipping through my fingers. Believing I had to be perfect in order to be loved. Believing I had to be perfect in order to be seen. Believing I had to be perfect at all. Skipping therapy. Putting the bare minimum on a pedestal. Apologizing to someone who owed me the apology. Not apologizing to someone I definitely should have. Not forgiving myself sooner. Pretending not to give a damn about the things I care deeply about. ***Forgetting I'm allowed to be human.***

SELF-LOVE REMINDER #4

You are not the things that keep you awake at night. You are not the mistakes you have made. You are not the hurt you have endured. You are not the love you have lost. You are not your tired bones. These things are part of you, but they are not all of you. Be careful of what you let define you.

How To Heal From The Things You Can't Forget

Understand that the deeper you push the aching down, the further it becomes implanted in your veins. Instead, remember it. **All of it.** The betrayals, the unfairness, the heart-shattering. Call your anguish to the forefront of your mind and retrace your steps to the places and people, and moments that broke you down. Allow your haunting to take a seat at the table. No, not just allow; invite the ghosts to sit right next to you. Coax the skeletons out of your closet and pull the monsters out from under your bed. Ask your demons what they have just been *dying* to tell you. **This part is important:** Listen to the story they tell you, and listen carefully because soon you will recognize it was your voice all along. Take your power back by rewriting the narrative. Realize you are still standing despite the wreckage. Realize there is so much damn beauty in the defiance of your own two feet. Realize that time does not heal all wounds, but what we do while the clock moves forward might.

An Incomplete List Of Reasons To Stay

Because you have so much left to learn. Because you haven't met your new best friend. Because you deserve to heal. Because you deserve your own love. Because you deserve to be here. Because the storm always passes. Because you have infinite potential to be discovered. Because summer is on its way. Because winter becomes magical to you again. Because you haven't finished writing your novel (and a little girl you'll never meet needs it). Because of art. Because of your dog. Because of your chosen family (by blood or otherwise). Because shit gets better. Because you haven't been to Ireland. Because feelings aren't facts. Because you are someone's proof that goodness still exists in people. Because you're important. Because you haven't seen Springsteen On Broadway in person yet. Because you're about to find a book that shifts your perspective on everything. Because you figure it out. Because you matter. Because you are loved. Because you are needed. Because what you think is unforgivable about you is not as bad as you think. Because you're allowed to be imperfect. ***Because it's not time to go.***

Some Better Things To Do Besides Texting Your Ex

Dance to Rihanna in the kitchen. Call your mom just to say you love her. Rearrange your room. Choose yourself. Swipe on Hinge. Pretend you never met them, even if it's just for a night. Understand that sometimes faking it until you make it actually works. Put away your phone. Put on an outfit that makes you feel beautiful. Put yourself out there. Draft what you wish you could say to them in the notes app and then delete it in the morning. Take a step back. Take a chance. Take the long way home after work and cry. Remember who you are. Remember who they are. Remember, this is why you broke up. Text your best friend and say why you're grateful for them. Look at the moon. Marvel at the stars. Read about the vastness of outer space and consider it a metaphor for your ability to love again. Rearrange your room. Cuddle your dog. Journal. Count your blessings in disguise, including your breakup. Take a nice, hot shower. Light a candle. Dig deep. Do the task you've been putting off for months that will take five minutes (yes, that one). Be grateful you collided with someone who made you feel so deeply once. Be glad you get another shot at the real thing. Understand the purpose they served. Go on a long, meandering walk and be humbled by the fact that the world has continued on despite them leaving yours. Go on a date with someone new. Let go. Give yourself the closure you wish they gave you.

Just Some Things That Make You Human

How your mind can paint a picture of a world that only exists in a fantasy book. Your beating heart. Saying the wrong thing. Missing the bus. Missing the point. Missing the person who broke you. Tired bones. Heavy eyes. Getting fired. Standing back up. Fidgeting. Stuttering during a meeting with your boss. Wishing you were someone else. Contemplating everything you would have had to miss if you actually *were* someone else. Realizing you actually don't want to be anyone else but you. Forgetting the same thing over and over. Relearning the hard lessons. Gratitude. Crying over a math test. Being overwhelmed by outer space and the ocean and what happens when we pass away. Getting your heart broken. Breaking someone else's heart. Believing it's been the end when it was simply a closed door. Self-pity. Listlessness. Jealousy. Inappropriate laughter in the funeral home. Goosebumps. Regret. Realizing what Bon Iver meant when he sang, "*At once I knew I was not magnificent.*" Struggling to say no. Struggling to say yes. Tripping in the parking lot. Cold feet. Daydreaming at work. Getting turned down. Getting turned on. Crying when your favorite character dies in a movie. Anger. Stretch marks. Curiosity. Wanting too much. Not wanting enough. Unrealistic expectations. Accidentally saying "shit" in front of kids at the grocery store. Getting ignored in the group chat. Doing your best and still not getting the results you hoped for. Figuring it out despite that fact. ***Your heart's ability to always have more room: For love. For loss. For dogs. For hope. For fear. For living.***

SELF-LOVE REMINDER #5

You are not perfect. You are **human**. And that is far more interesting, anyway.

Rules For Living Well

Speak up when you're hurt. Slow down when you're happy. Trust good things when they come along. Wear the crop top. Give yourself more credit. Forgive what needs forgiveness, including yourself. Take the chance. Eat the pasta. Be kind, even when it's hard (especially then). Work like hell on what matters to you. Cut the excess. Dabble in overindulgence every now and then, too. Tell someone when you love them (even if they don't necessarily feel it back). Hope for the best but accept whatever happens anyway. Lean into the present moment as often as you can. Sweat it out. Cry it out. Let it go. Spend enough time alone. Become someone you can call a friend. Put yourself out there. Admit when you fucked up. Stop over-explaining your heart to those committed to misunderstanding it. Offer a hand to those who need it. Ask for help when that person is you. Pick your battles. Choose your family. Buy jeans in your actual size, not your "goal" size. Retire the idea of a "goal" size at all. Allow room for messiness. Read what you actually like, not what you think you *should* be reading. Define success on your own terms. Listen to the music that feels like home. Listen to the people who feel like magic. Listen to your heart because you deserve to hear what it has to say. Feel everything it is you do. Life is short. You might as well experience it fully while you're here.

The Different Ways You Abandon Yourself

Saying "yes" when you're aching to say "no." Apologizing to someone who owes *you* the apology. Digging your heels in deeper when you know *you're* the one in the wrong. Over-explaining your truth to someone who stopped listening a long time ago. Romanticizing the bare minimum. Begging for basic decency. Chasing people who do not want to be caught. Building a life based on what you think looks "good" but not on what actually *feels* good. Ignoring your intuition. Ignoring your body. Ignoring your needs. Contorting and bending and breaking to fit in places you know you've outgrown. Staying in a relationship that has run its course. Not allowing time for deep rest. Running on fumes. Staying quiet when someone disrespects you. Refusing to allow what already is. Lying to yourself. Never asking for help. Never taking a chance on yourself. Never living up to your own word. Celebrating those who only tolerate you. ***Wishing you were someone else.***

Short Success Stories

Landing the role at your dream company you've wanted since you were 22 at 29. Working a job just to pay the damn bills. Raising the kind kids you've wanted to have since you can remember. Deciding parenthood isn't for you and traveling the world instead. Paying off your last credit card bill in full. Finishing your manuscript. Forgiving yourself. Quitting a vice. Trying again after getting knocked down. Breaking the cycles of past generations. Adopting the dog you've dreamt about since you were a kid. Admitting you need help. Getting into college. Deciding against higher education to pursue makeup artistry instead. Moving out of your parents' house. Cutting ties with an ex. Living a life that could only be described as your own.

An Incomprehensive List Of Things That Aren't As Shameful As You Think

Drunk texting your ex. Calling it an early night while everyone else goes to the next bar. Asking for help even if you technically could do something on your own. Forgetting a deadline. Admitting you're depressed and afraid. Admitting you're so lonely you can't stand it. Admitting you fucked up and don't know how to make it right. Crying in front of someone you don't know particularly well. Oversharing on a first date. Getting ghosted. Telling a joke only the crickets find funny. Telling your therapist you want to increase your sessions. Telling your secrets to someone who didn't care enough to keep them. Falling for a friend you know deep down doesn't feel the same but revealing your feelings anyway. Getting rejected. Credit card debt. Monthly prescriptions for fluoxetine. Not knowing what you want to do next. Going up a size in jeans. Being the weird, hyper kid growing up. Anything that you're thinking about right now. You're not so bad. You're human. ***Allow yourself to be so.***

SELF-LOVE REMINDER #6

Stop chasing what only keeps you running. Stop chasing anything that makes you question your worth. Stop watering yourself down for people who don't want to see you bloom.

Some Shit That Is More Interesting Than "Perfection"

Skinned knees. Beauty marks. Appendicitis scars. An authentic albeit messy human. Curse words. Chipped nail polish. Trying to relearn German and realizing you never really knew the language in the first place. The hope of trying "again" anyway. Crinkly eyes. Chapped lips. Weathered hands. Understanding there are so many stories you will never know. Understanding there are so many soulmates you will never know. Understanding there is so much annoying shit about you that you will never know. Deep connection. Learning something the hard way. Stretch marks. A gap in between two front teeth. A constellation of freckles. Tan lines in a wedding gown. Sunburned shoulders. Your past. Your future. Your present moment. Rejection. Heartbreak. One-sided closure. Forgiving someone who doesn't necessarily deserve it. Unfinished sentences. Unfinished basements. Unfinished people. Snort laughs. Goofy mistakes. A sprinkle of faux pas here and there. A burned ego. Typos. The first draft. The unedited truth. ***Someone seeing your fault lines and saying they have them, too.***

It's not your responsibility to…

Soften your edges. Manage emotions that are not your own. Bend until you break for the sake of another's convenience. Shrink to make room for others' insecurities. Remain in spaces you have long outgrown. Remain in relationships because of shared history. Remain quiet when disrespected in order to "keep the peace." Give away your time to those who have shown they do not value it. Forgive someone who clearly isn't sorry. Explain your heart to someone who will never speak its language. Negotiate your worth. Read minds. Be accessible all the time. Be everything to everyone. ***Be anything other than human.***

Things That Improved My Life For The Better

Deep breathing. Deep conversations over coffee. Deep feeling. Finding a therapist I actually worked well with. Expressing my needs (even if they weren't going to be met) because they still deserved to be heard. Cutting ties with people who would never understand my heart simply because they did not want to. Cutting ties with people who did not understand my words because they weren't listening in the first place. Cutting ties with versions of myself I no longer relate to. Giving those past selves grace anyway. Making a point to check out the golden-hour sky. Being intentional with who gets my time. Being intentional with who hears my stories. Being intentional with most things, really. Slowing down. Finally getting the dog. Counting to 10 before reacting. Remembering that the people who passed on will find ways to show you they're still with you. Saying it plain. When I stopped trying to make him care. When I stopped trying to be someone I'm not. When I stopped expecting the worst and began wondering what the best would look like instead.

You Deserve More Than...

Half-assed effort. Apologies without changed behavior. Your negative self-talk. Being left on read for a week by someone who supposedly likes you. Being treated like a convenience. Being treated like a trial run. Pretending to be someone you're not because you think that this person is more worth loving than who you actually are. Not speaking your truth. Not stepping into your power. Not giving yourself a chance. Refusing to do something you know will better your life because you're convinced you don't actually deserve to be happy. Not honoring how you feel. Constantly waiting for the other shoe to drop. Always assuming the worst. The bare minimum. Unmatched energy. Fair-weather friends. Rude dates. People who have decided they do not care to understand you. Staying in places you know you have outgrown. Staying at a party you're not having fun at. Staying quiet when you're aching to be heard. Living a life you know isn't actually your own.

SELF-LOVE REMINDER #7

Be brave enough to let
yourself be sad over
something that mattered.

Shit Life Is Just Too Damn Short For

Not wearing the crop top. Not saying "I love you" when you experience it. Not sending the risky text. Postponing feeling alive for Saturday night or summer or when you're 10 pounds smaller. Editing out how you really feel. Refusing to apologize because you're too hellbent on being "right." Holding grudges. Holding onto the past. Holding back your tears. Finishing the movie you don't care for. Looking at life as a series of checkboxes. Skipping the party because your ex is there. Analyzing your mind and yourself and your life so much you neglect to live at all. Passing on the pasta dish. Worrying about the people who don't like you instead of focusing on the ones who adore you. Worrying so much about being liked that you act like someone you aren't. Believing striving for perfection is a worthy endeavor. Stifling a laugh. Being afraid to take up space. Being afraid of making mistakes you don't try at all. Forgetting to look up at the night sky. Living in what-ifs instead of what-is. **Love (but you need to keep loving anyway).**

Things That Will Always Restore Your Energy

80-degree weather. The sun dancing down your back. The wind whispering secrets in your ears. The grass tickling the bottoms of your bare feet. A glass of ice-cold water after a sweaty workout. Snuggles from your dog. Speaking up for what you know to be true. Letting go of what no longer serves you. Letting some shit be. Letting yourself be seen as all that you are. Singing in the car. Picking up the tab for a friend going through a rough time. A hug when you really need it. Swimming among Lake Michigan's waves at the beginning of August. Working like hell on something you care deeply about. Listening. Asking for help. Asking more questions. Asking what you can do for someone else. Random wine nights. Long, meandering walks with someone you love. Watching two people you adore get married. Dancing until 2 AM. Sleeping until your body actually feels rested. Apologizing. Reading a new book that captures your heart. Putting away your phone. Therapy. Forgetting yourself every now and then. Doing the right thing quietly. Radical acceptance. Staying close to anyone who makes you believe in the good of people. ***Doing more of what makes you feel utterly and frantically alive.***

SELF-LOVE REMINDER #8

Love yourself more
than you love the idea
of someone else.

Vital Signs

The rhythm of your heartbeat. The pattern of your breath. Your willingness to keep trying. Your ability to imagine more for yourself. Sensitivity to light. Fear that creeps slowly up your spine. Intrigue that captures your eyes. Faith. A broken heart. Reflexes. Rage. Seeing that there is something to stay for. Knowing there is always something more. Staying, staying, staying.

Legacies To Leave Behind

How kind you remained when the world was not so kind to you. How patient you were. How stubborn your faith in goodness was. How you made others feel about themselves. Healing your heart. A blueprint for a better world. Radical gentleness. Reckless hopefulness. The idea that perfection is boring. Wisdom that could only be gleaned from your unique existence. Telling the truth, even when it's hard. Showing up, even when it's hard. Being a person, even when it's hard loving yourself and others, even when it feels impossible.

MOLLY BURFORD is a writer from Detroit. Her work aims to capture the human condition in all of its forms including the beautiful, the painful, the ugly, the goofy, and all of those in-between parts we try and hide away. *Moments To Hold Close* is Burford's first poetry collection.

You can find Burford on Instagram at @mollyburford, on Twitter @mburf92, or at mollyburford.com.

If you have tips for her on how to meet Pete Davidson or other general inquiries, you can email her at: burfordmolly@gmail.com.

More from
Thought Catalog Books

A Gentle Reminder
—Bianca Sparacino

When You're Ready, This Is How You Heal
—Brianna Wiest

Everything You'll Ever Need
(You Can Find Within Yourself)
—Charlotte Freeman

Holding Space for the Sun
—Jamal Cadoura

All That You Deserve
—Jacqueline Whitney

How Does It Feel?
—Andrew Kearns

THOUGHT
CATALOG
Books

THOUGHTCATALOG.COM